Above: Grammar holding the key to the door of the seven Liberal Arts.
From Margarita Philosophica by Gregor Reisch, 1508.

First published 2012
This edition © Wooden Books Ltd 2012

Published by Wooden Books Ltd.
8A Market Place, Glastonbury, Somerset

British Library Cataloguing in Publication Data
Grenon, R.
Grammar

A CIP catalogue record for this book is
available from the British Library

ISBN 978 1 904263 68 5

Printed and bound in Shanghai, China
by Shanghai iPrinting Co., Ltd.
100% recycled papers.

GRAMMAR

THE STRUCTURE OF LANGUAGE

by

Rachel Grenon

To Pierre

Thanks to Jan Suchanek, Amy Klement and Earl Fontainelle for extra materials and edits. Special thanks to Paul Taylor at the Warburg Institute for assistance with picture research. Perspective letter engravings from Perspectiva Literaria *by Johannes Lencker, Nuremberg, 1567, and* Praxis Perspectivae *by Lucas Brunn, Nuremberg, 1615, both in* Fantastic Geometry *by David Wade, 2012. For further reading try* The Complete Guide to Grammar, *by Rosalind Fergusson and Martin H. Manser,* The Bloomsbury Grammar Guide *by Gordon Jarvie,* Everyday Grammar *by John Seely, and* The Oxford Companion to the English Language.

Above: Pronouns and Adverbs, from Gymnastica Literaria, *by Nicolaus Valla, Venice, 1516*

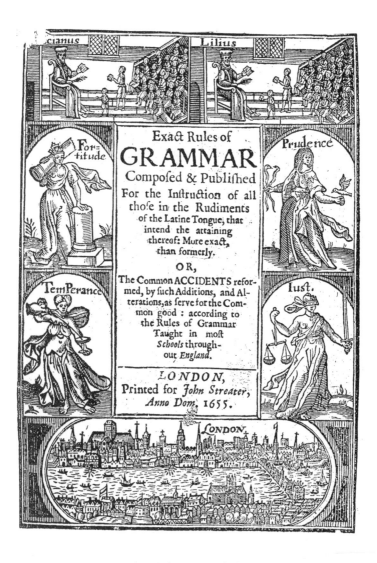

Prifcianus

Lilius

For=
titude

Prudence

TemPerance

Iust.

Exact Rules of
GRAMMAR

Composed & Published

For the Instruction of all
those in the Rudiments
of the Latine Tongue, that
intend the attaining
thereof: More exact,
than formerly.

OR,

The Common ACCIDENTS refor-
med, by such Additions, and Al-
terations, as serve for the Common good : according to
the Rules of Grammar
Taught in most
Schools through-
out *England.*

LONDON,
Printed for *John Streater,*
Anno Dom. 1655.

LONDON

INTRODUCTION

If you are reading this book, you already have some notion of grammar. As your eyes skim the page, your brain gleans some meaning from the symbols printed upon it. You understand that the words must come in a certain order, that some words denote things whilst others denote actions, and that different types of words fulfil different functions.

Language, governed by a complex system of symbols and rules, is humanity's vehicle for thought and communication. The possession of grammar and syntax is thus one of the most distinctive features of the human race.

This book is designed as a short introduction into the philosophy of grammar and language in general, and on English grammar and lexic in particular. Understanding the rules which govern our vehicle of thought can make it much easier to acquire foreign languages, as well as liberating our thinking itself. Thousands of languages are still spoken on Earth and many people frequently use more than one. Some languages have similar rules, and probably common ancestors, and to understand the rules that govern the English language, we will be looking further than English. In the ancient scholarly curriculum, grammar forms part of the *Trivium,* with its sister sciences of *logic* and *rhetoric.* Logic asks: *when is a sentence true?* Rhetoric asks: *which is the right sentence?* Grammar purely asks: *when is a sentence correct?*

Despite the tiny size of the book, I am nonetheless hopeful that these pages will at least whet your appetite for grammar, if not turn you into a most ardent and impassioned grammarian.

STARTING WITH WRITING
alphabet systems and languages

The word GRAMMAR comes from the Greek term *gramma* (a letter), itself related to *grapho* (to draw or write). The invention of SCRIPT, around 3000 BC in Sumeria and India, suddenly made it possible to write and read texts of law, commerce, ritual, poetry, history, philosophy and science. And, perhaps most important of all, it gave birth to the detailed discussion of the *correct form* of such texts.

Broadly speaking, scripts come in two types. LOGOGRAPHIC systems try to depict the *meaning* of a text without relating to the sound of language; the CHINESE SCRIPT being a prime example. PHONOGRAPHIC systems, on the other hand, record text as it would *sound* when spoken. The ROMAN ALPHABET, which we use to write English and other Western European tongues, is phonographic, as are the scripts used for *Hebrew, Russian, Greek, Arabic* and *Sanskrit*. Today's *International Phonetic Alphabet* is used for correctly writing the pronunciation of languages.

Every natural language uses a distinct set of sounds as building blocks, these generally being classified as either *consonants* or *vowels*. Distinguishing how and with which parts of our speech organs these sounds are formed can be of great help in the acquisition of a language. The science of sounds in speech and language is called PHONETICS.

漢 汉 **ABC** देवनागरी 𑀖𑀫 אלפבית ひ カ
字 字 **αλφάβητο Кириллица** أبجدية らカ
⠇⠑⠙ ตัวอักษรไทย ᚠᚢᚦᚨᚱᚲ 한글 な ナ

𒀭 𒅗 𒃲 𒁾 𒀀 𒉈 𒈝 𒌋 ᚠ ᚦ ᚷ ᛝ ᛋ ᛟ ᛞ ᛏ ᛗ

PETROGLYPH | HIEROGLYPH | SYLLABIC | A L P H A B E T S

PALEOLITHIC 15,000-12,000 B.C. STONE AGE / MESOLITHIC 12,000-7,000 B.C. NEOLITHIC 7,000-5,000 B.C. ARMENIA	CHALCOLITHIC ROCK CARVING COPPER-BRONZE AGE 5000-2000 B.C. ARMENIA	METZAMOR INSCRIPTION 2000-1800 B.C. / DRAMATIC STYLE SINGLE SIGN ARMENIA	NYSSOSIAN SINAI	MAINKAZIAN INSCRIPTION 1500 B.C. ARMENIA	URARTIAN INSCRIPTION 1790-1580 B.C. ARMENIA	ARMAVIR INSCRIPTION 1780 B.C. ARMENIA	CHOLAGERD 850-150 B.C. ARMENIA	URARTIAN CUNEIFORM 850-550 B.C. ARMENIA	NYSSOSIAN after 1700 B.C.	MAINKAZIAN OLD ARMENIAN 7-16th Cent.A.D. / CLASSICAL ERKATAGIR	ODESSIAN 3-14th Cent.B.C.	MESROBIAN 406 A.D. - PRESENT ARMENIA		NAME	PHONETIC VALUE

Left: Examples of various script forms, ancient and modern, from around the world.
Above: A suggestive interpretation of the evolution of the Armenian Indo-European alphabet.

3

EARLY GRAMMAR
Sanskrit, Greek, and Latin

One of the earliest written languages for which governing rules were established is Indian *Sanskrit* (Sanskrit hymns are among the oldest written texts on earth), and the first compilation of its rules was made by PANINI around 450 BC. One of the most prominent features of Sanskrit is *inflection,* where words *undergo changes* to express relationships. In English *he* might become *his* or *him,* and in Sanskrit *deva* means *god* while *devasya* means *of the god.* Sanskrit is the oldest recorded language of a branch of tongues called the *Indo-European Language Family.* Our own ancestors probably spoke a language very similar to Sanskrit.

The first concise grammar in the West is attributed to DIONYSIUS THRAX (170–90 BC), who taught in Alexandria, Egypt. He found that words in classical GREEK *change according to rules,* and when LATIN later came to dominate the Western world, scholars noticed that it too was similar. We now know that Sanskrit, Greek, and Latin share a common ancestor and that other members of this family include *Indo-Iranian, Balto-Slavic, Celtic* and *Germanic.* Although classical Latin disappeared, its dialects became today's Romance languages. This means that our language now has a quite extensive family tree.

Broadly speaking, older languages have more complex systems of inflection, while the grammar of younger languages is more simplified. Immigration, trade, invasions and occupations may have forced villagers to learn more languages over time, and, rather than mastering the intricacies of any particular tongue, they muddled along with a simplified speech which later became the rule. Perhaps the finest example of such a process and its result is English.

4

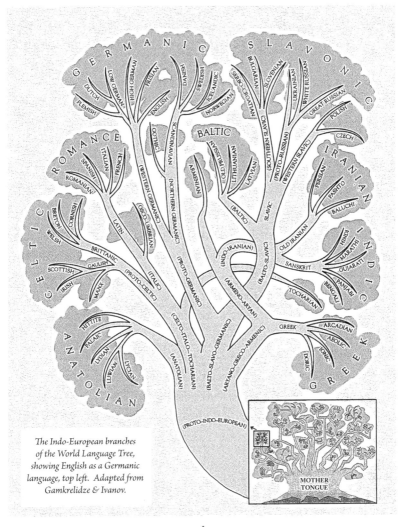

The Indo-European branches of the World Language Tree, showing English as a Germanic language, top left. Adapted from Gamkrelidze & Ivanov.

The labels on the tree include:

GERMANIC — FLEMISH, DUTCH, LOW GERMAN, HIGH GERMAN, FRISIAN, ENGLISH, DANISH, SWEDISH, ICELANDIC, NORWEGIAN, GOTHIC, SCANDINAVIAN, (WESTERN GERMANIC), (NORTHERN GERMANIC)

SLAVONIC — BULGARIAN, SERBO-CROATIAN, SLOVENIAN, (CHURCH SLAVONIC), UKRAINIAN, WHITE RUSSIAN, GREAT RUSSIAN, POLISH, CZECH, (SOUTHERN SLAVIC), (PROTO-RUSSIAN), (WESTERN SLAVIC)

BALTIC — OLD PRUSSIAN, LITHUANIAN, LATVIAN, ARMENIAN, SLAVIC, (BALTIC)

ROMANCE — ITALIAN, SPANISH, FRENCH, ROMANIAN, LATIN, (OSCO-UMBRIAN)

IRANIAN — PERSIAN, PASHTO, BALUCHI, OLD IRANIAN

INDIC — HINDI, MARATHI, GUJARATI, PANJABI, BENGALI, SANSKRIT, TOCHARIAN

CELTIC — BRETON, CORNISH, WELSH, BRITTANIC, SCOTTISH, GAULISH, IRISH, MANX, (PROTO-CELTIC)

ANATOLIAN — HITTITE, PALAIC, LYDIAN, LUVIAN, LYCIAN

GREEK — ARCADIAN, AEOLIC, IONIC, DORIC

(ITALIC), (PROTO-GERMANIC), (INDO-IRANIAN), (BALTO-SLAVIC), (ARMENO-ARYAN), (CELTO-ITALO-TOCHARIAN), (BALTO-SLAVO-GERMANIC), (ARYANO-GRECO-ARMENIC), (ANATOLIAN), (PROTO-INDO-EUROPEAN)

MOTHER TONGUE

5

THE STORY OF ENGLISH
a rich and diverse heritage

The British Isles, at the northwestern tip of the European peninsula of the Eurasian continent, have experienced many waves of immigration in their long history, both as invasions and peaceful settlements. The first settlers arrived in the early Stone Age, and of their language we have no trace. However, at the time of the Roman conquest, we know that Celtic languages were spoken. Then, after the Romans departed in AD 410, a huge wave of Anglo-Saxon immigration from what is now northern Germany brought with it a language known as OLD SAXON, with many of the words we use today. In addition, plundering, settlement, and trading by Norsemen also brought in further foreign words, resulting in the fascinating blend of OLD ENGLISH.

Just as the language was beginning to settle down, the Norman conquest of 1066 brought in a plethora of new FRENCH terms which soon changed the language forever. French words in English include *judge, government, brunette, nation, parliament, voyage, president, route, inhabitant, arrive.* Luckily, Norman French and Old English broadly shared the rules of inflection common to all Indo-European tongues, but their two systems were still somewhat incompatible, so most people soon began to ignore both systems, resulting in the fact that there is little inflectional grammar left at all in English today. MODERN ENGLISH thus emerged as a hybrid language, about 26% Germanic, 29% Latin, 29% French, 6% Greek, 4% proper names and 6% from elsewhere. It continues today to absorb and transmit words, and its grammar and pronunciation remain *in flux.* It now functions primarily through the combination of predominantly inflexible words, making the language relatively similar to CHINESE in this respect.

Above: The primary distribution of native language across the planet. Notice the language island Finland and Estonia create within the Indo-European grouping. Note too Madagascar.

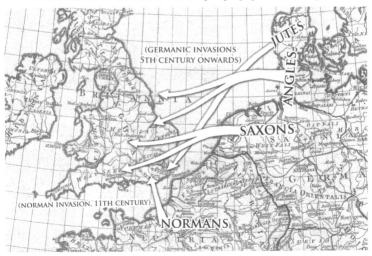

Above: The main waves of peoples that resulted in the English language. The Celtic languages, once spoken throughout this same area, are today confined to the extremities.

MAKING SENSE
putting words together

Languages combine sounds to express meanings, and GRAMMAR describes the rules of this process. There are at least five different ways to do this:

COMBINATION. For example, the sounds *un* and *lock* can be combined creating the new word *unlock*.

COMBINATION USING CONNECTING WORDS. For example, the words *key* and *lock* can be combined using a preposition: *key in lock*.

WORD ORDER. Obviously, *hole in wall* has a different meaning to *wall in hole*. Languages that use a lot of inflection, like Sanskrit or Russian, have a less strict word order, while English makes heavy use of word order—compare *Tom sees Anya* to *Anya sees Tom*.

ACCENT, STRESS, INTONATION, AND PITCH. Modern Indo-European languages use changes in stress, intonation or pitch to convey emotional content, or to denote a question. In languages such as Chinese, however, the same syllable can have completely different meanings depending on the shape of the gradient in the pitch of the voice.

INFLECTION. Here, the word is slightly altered to express a different relation; e.g. the word *see* can be inflected to *saw*, conveying a different temporal aspect. The Indo-European languages all share the same rules on how to inflect both nouns (called *declension*) and verbs (called *conjugation*), with some variation between them. English has lost much of this over time. For example, the old intimate second person singular *thou* has been largely dropped. In Middle English it once became *thee* for the accusative and dative, and *thy* or *thine* for the possesive.

The example below shows how the conjugations of the verb *to make* have changed in English over the centuries.

OLD ENGLISH	MIDDLE ENGLISH	TODAY'S ENGLISH
ich make	*I make*	*I make*
þu makest	*thou makst*	*you make*
he makeþ	*he maketh*	*he makes*
we maken	*we make*	*we make*
ge maken	*ye make*	*you make*
hio maken	*they make*	*they make*

And here is another example, showing how the declensions of the noun angel have likewise changed over time.

	LATIN	OLD ENGLISH	TODAY
NOMINATIVE (I, *angel*)	*angelus*	*engel*	*angel*
ACCUSATIVE (I saw the *angel*)	*angelum*	*engel*	*angel*
GENITIVE (my, his, *angel*)	*angeli*	*engles*	*angel*
DATIVE (to the *angel*)	*angelo*	*engle*	*angel*

English, in fact, is becoming more and more like Chinese, which uses no inflection and is comprised of one-syllable particles—similar to the following English sentence: *"He has got to go for this, hey, you must see it's not so hard to do"*. So, in English, many of the early grammatical rules today explain the exceptions, rather than serving as rules, and declension remains, for the most part, merely in the personal pronouns. An exception is the genitive, which remains as *'s*, the apostrophe indicating where the *e* dropped out, as in *engles* (*above*), so today *it is the angel's*.

CATEGORIES & TERMS
the five building blocks

Language can communicate both *thoughts* and *emotions,* but while emotions can also be conveyed by music or facial expressions, thoughts are more intrinsically linked to language and the use of symbols. When a word is not just a combination of sounds, but has a certain meaning, it is called a *term*. Speakers and listeners who agree on the meaning of a word have *come to terms*—they understand what they are talking about. Each term can be expanded or refined, and set in relation to other terms.

There are different types of terms: those which describe *objects*, those which describe *actions,* and those which *quantify relations*. Thus at the earliest level of language there are words that are learned as the names of observed objects, as well as words that name abstract things which cannot be pointed at physically but that are explained by words learned earlier, such as *the mind*. Then there are words that can be demonstrated, actions that later expand to actions that cannot be demonstrated, such as *to postpone*. Finally, there are many words that create relations, such as *with* or *behind*, most of which we learn by example.

We have reason to suspect that there is a fundamental difference between an object and an action, between a location and a quality, and different types of relation in time, space, and in causation. These are philosophical categories too—not just grammatical. The observation of different categories of terms was at the beginning of a whole tradition of philosophy, asking how fundamental these categories are, starting with Aristotle (384–322 BC). *Substance* and *action*, as expressed by *noun* and *verb* phrases, indeed seem categorical. Then there are classes of *qualities* and *relations*.

It is useful to classify terms according to the categories they belong to, and different grammatical rules often apply to these different classes.

A NOUN is a word standing for something at which we can point. Such a term evokes a picture of a substance in the mind, such as tree; this is not a specific tree, but a general idea. Some qualities are intrinsic to the idea tree and can be listed in a definition.

A VERB is a predicate to a substantive or noun, as it describes the action concerning or linking one or more substance, e.g. *the tree grows*. Actions are always associated with substances—in most cases they are what speech is really about. In the sentence *the man drives a car* there are two such substances: *the man*, and *the car*. One is *subject* to the action, in this case, the man: what he is and does is here completely determined by the act of driving. The other is *object* to the action, in this case, the car: it is controlled by the action, but is also challenging the action, as it needs to be controlled.

There are thus five main building blocks of language (*italicised below*). English grammar also works at five levels: SENTENCES are made up of CLAUSES, which are made up of PHRASES, which consist of WORDS, which are composed of MORPHEMES.

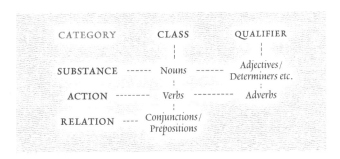

CLASSIFYING WORDS
parts of speech

ARISTOTLE (384–322 BC) listed only NOUNS and VERBS as parts of speech. Since the first grammarians were occupied with the differences between *substance* and *action,* this led to an extensive discussion in philosophy. Are these categories somehow more fundamental than grammar itself? A substance, for example, appears timeless while a verb, in contrast, always happens in time. In English grammar, words are commonly grouped into nine classes (parts of speech) in two categories:

OPEN: NOUNS – naming words
           PRONOUNS – words that stand in for nouns
           ADJECTIVES – modify nouns
           MAIN VERBS – express actions and states
           ADVERBS – modify verbs, adjectives or other adverbs

CLOSED: DETERMINERS – modify nouns
           PRONOUNS – stand in for nouns
           CONJUNCTIONS – connecting words
           PREPOSITIONS – show the relationship between words

Open words are *content* words and carry the meaning of a sentence. Closed words are the *function* or *structure* words of a sentence. The closed classes are limited, rarely admitting new words, while the open classes readily do so, e.g. the new noun *locavore* (one who eats locally grown food).

Throughout this book, we will explore the nature and function of these word classes.

The investigation of the meaning of words is the beginning of education. — Antisthenes

DETERMINERS
identify yourself

I *pass by* THESE *walls,* THE *walls of Layla*
And I kiss THIS *wall and* THAT *wall*
It's *not Love of* THE *houses that has taken* MY *heart*
But *of* THE *One who dwells in* THOSE *houses*

poem attributed to Qays ibn al-Mulawwah

DETERMINERS come before nouns and tell us something about their number, definiteness, proximity and ownership. Classes of determiners:

DEFINITE ARTICLE – *the*
INDEFINITE ARTICLE – *a/an, any, some, that, those, this, whichever, whatever*
DEMONSTRATIVE DETERMINERS – *this, that, these, those*
POSSESSIVE DETERMINERS – *my, your, his, her, its, our, their*
RELATIVE DETERMINERS – *whose, whichever, whatever*
INTERROGATIVE DETERMINERS – *whose, which, what*
S-GENITIVE – *Harold's*
NUMERALS – *Cardinal and ordinal numerals before a noun;*
            two donkeys, *first* night

THE NOUN PHRASE
a thing of substance

The noun phrase within a sentence is a word or a group of words describing something of substance (rather than an action), e.g. *the horse*, or *the tall horse*. At its core is usually a substantive or noun, *horse* or *Peter*, or a pronoun that has taken its place, e.g. *it* or *he*. Rules now apply.

Logical rules deal with the content of the words, and so with terms rather than words. For example, *the black sun* would be illogical, since there is only one sun and it is clearly not black. Some qualities are also intrinsic to nouns and need not be specified once we understand the term. A statement such as *the sphere is round* is an ANALYTICAL STATEMENT, and basically redundant if we know what we are talking about.

Grammatical rules deal with certain qualities the words carry. For example, the word *house* conveys the fact that a singular object is being discussed; while in the word *houses* the annexed *s* denotes a plurality. In the inflecting Indo-European languages, substantives carry three such intrinsic qualities, *number*, *gender* and *case*:

NUMBER, e.g. *house/houses*. While English only uses singular and plural, some Indo-European languages also have a duality declension, for things appearing in pairs, a bit like *the twain*, or *a pair of scissors* or *trousers*.

GENDER, e.g. *priest/priestess*. Grammatical gender is not the same thing as the sex of an object. English does not use gender, and preserves the concept only in very few words. However, other Indo-European languages have two, or even three genders. In German, for example, *der Mond* (the moon) is masculine, while *das Mädchen* (the maiden) is neuter.

CASE, e.g. *Peter/Peter's* (genitive). Here, the word gets slightly altered to express a certain function or relation it is performing in the clause. In English, there are only nominative and genitive, however older Indo-European languages may possess all or some of the following cases:

NOMINATIVE – the term is the agent of an action; *the horse* ran.

GENITIVE – the term is possessor of another term; *the horses'* stable.

DATIVE – the term is receiver of something or indirect object of an action; to give something *to the horse.*

ACCUSATIVE – the term is the direct object of an action; to ride *the horse.*

ABLATIVE – the term is the origin of the action; he ran *from the horse.*

INSTRUMENTAL – the term is tool of an action; to ride a horse *with a saddle.*

LOCATIVE – the term is the location of something; to ride *on the path.*

VOCATIVE – the term is directly addressed; *o! horse!*

The word *horse* does not change in these English examples, but consider Latin: *equuus* (nom); *equui* (gen); *equuo* (dat); *equum* (acc); *eque* (voc), or German: *das Pferd, des Pferdes, dem Pferde, das Pferd.* In the noun phrase the noun and all extensions of the noun (i.e. the determiner and adjectives) must agree in case, gender, and number, e.g. in French *la maison verte* (the green house), *le tapis vert* (the green cover).

These noun changes are known as DECLENSION. In English, declension is limited to SINGULAR *vs.* PLURAL number (*cat/cats*) and NOMINATIVE *vs.* GENITIVE case (*the cat* or *the cat's*). There are, however, some exceptions, as a few nouns do take GENDER forms (*prince/princess*) while others are sometimes considered female (*ship/moon*).

ENGLISH NOUNS
the name of the game

As illustrated by the emphasised words below, NOUNS take many different forms. Nouns form the largest part of the English vocabulary.

When ICICLES hang by the WALL
    And DICK the SHEPHERD blows his NAIL,
And TOM bears LOGS into the HALL,
    And MILK comes frozen HOME in PAIL;

When BLOOD is nipt and WAYS be foul,
    Then nightly sings the staring OWL
Tuwhoo! Tuwhit! Tuwhoo! A merry NOTE!
    While greasy JOAN doth keel the POT.

When all aloud the WIND doth blow
    And COUGHING drowns the PARSON's SAW,
And BIRDS sit brooding in the SNOW,
    And MARIAN's NOSE looks red and raw;

When roasted CRABS hiss in the BOWL
    Then nightly sings the staring OWL
Tuwhoo! Tuwhit! Tuwhoo! A merry NOTE!
    While greasy JOAN doth keel the POT.

William Shakespeare

Nouns name people, things, places or ideas that are:

ANIMATE	INANIMATE
Joan, parson, owl	*pail, snow, logs, fork, newspaper*
CONCRETE	ABSTRACT
milk, bread, piano, music	*freedom, anger, happiness, glory*

PROPER NOUNS refer to persons, places, geographical features, or various periods of time; *William Shakespeare, Marian, Asia, the Amazon River, Sunday.*

COMMON NOUNS refer to general entities. Most common nouns have a singular and a plural form; *crab/crabs, rose/roses, liberty/liberties, man/men, child/children.*

COUNT NOUNS denote things that can be counted; one *person*, two *glasses*, many *problems*, several *books.*

NONCOUNT (OR MASS) NOUNS refer to inanimate entities or constructs and are usually only expressed in singular form; *thunder, cotton, milk, luggage, hair.*

COLLECTIVE NOUNS define groups composed of individual members referred to collectively; *team, class, electorate, parliament, flock, herd, army.*

PRONOUNS
standing in

PRONOUNS are words that stand in for nouns or other pronouns. They allow us to refer to a word that has already been mentioned without having to repeat it. Pronouns can also be used to refer to people or things which have no antecedent in the text. PERSONAL PRONOUNS refer to the people or things involved in a text, and change to reflect person, number, gender and case.

SUBJECTIVE	OBJECTIVE	REFLEXIVE	POSSESSIVE
I	Me	*Myself*	My
You	You	*Yourself*	Your
He/She/It	Him/Her/It	*Him/Her/Itself*	His/Hers/Its
We	Us	*Ourselves*	Our
You	You	*Yourselves*	Your
They	Them	*Themselves*	Their

SUBJECTIVE PRONOUNS act as the *subject* of a sentence or clause,

> I'm nobody! Who are YOU?
> Are YOU nobody, too?

OBJECTIVE PRONOUNS are used as the *object* of a sentence or clause.

> Then there's a pair of US–don't tell!
> They'd banish US, you know.

Emily Dickinson

REFLEXIVE PRONOUNS are used when the object of the sentence is the same as the subject, and can also be used for emphasis.

> I am, indeed, a king, because I know how to rule MYSELF. — Pietro Aretino

> If you make YOURSELF understood, you're always speaking well. — Molière

POSSESSIVE PRONOUNS show personal possession. They substitute for a possessive adjective and a noun.

His money is twice tainted: 'taint YOURS and 'taint MINE. — Mark Twain

Other types of pronouns include:

RECIPROCAL PRONOUNS, which express mutual action or relationship, in English *each other*, or *one another*.

Words are but symbols for the relations of things to ONE ANOTHER and to us;
nowhere do they touch upon absolute truth. — Friedrich Nietzsche

DEMONSTRATIVE PRONOUNS identify nouns; *this, that, these, those, such.*

There are three classes of people: THOSE who see, THOSE who see when
they are shown, THOSE who do not see. — Leonardo da Vinci

Always do right. THIS will gratify some people and astonish the rest. — Mark Twain

SUCH as we are made of, SUCH we be. — William Shakespeare

INTERROGATIVE PRONOUNS are used to ask questions; *who, what, why,*
where, when, whatever.

WHAT's in a name? That which we call a rose
By any other name would smell as sweet. — William Shakespeare

INDEFINITE PRONOUNS refer to people or things in a vague or general way;
any, anything, anybody, anyone, some, something, somebody, someone, none, no one,
nothing, nobody, none, either, neither, both, each, all, everything, everybody, everyone.

Trying to please EVERYBODY, I pleased NOBODY. — Richard Wright

RELATIVE PRONOUNS introduce relative clauses (*see page 53*). They refer to
a noun that has already been mentioned, and give more information about
it; *who, whose, whom* are used for people, *which, what, that* refer to things.

The person, be it gentleman or lady, WHO has not pleasure in a good
novel, must be intolerably stupid. — Jane Austin

Knowledge WHICH is acquired under compulsion obtains no hold on the mind. — Plato

ADJECTIVES
enriching the qualities of substance

Every noun evokes an idea, the essence of its term, so the essence (or definition) of *wine*, is *alcoholic beverage made by the fermentation of grape juice*. Plato thought of nouns as representing *ideas* rather than *things* and nouns demonstrate that the easiest way to evoke a thought about something is to name it, so if I say *Shakespeare*, you may immediately visualise someone. This does not work, however, with general words like *cat*, or abstract concepts like *reality*. If, for example, I say *woman*, of whom am I speaking? We need some quality or relation to distinguish her. Is she perhaps *the tall woman in the red dress on the left*? Grammatically, the noun phrase has expanded around the noun *woman* using attributives, *tall*, *in the red dress*, *on the left*.

The most common ways of expanding NOUN PHRASES are:

ARTICLES: These are particles that precede a noun, such as *the* tree, or *a* tree (compare with *such trees* or *any tree*). The main function of articles is to define whether we are talking about one specific element of the idea, *the car* or *their car*, or any member, *a car*.

DECLENSION: As we saw earlier (*pages 14–15*), many languages (English not really among them) include certain qualities in a noun's declension, which must agree in *number*, *gender*, and *case*, so for example *goose/geece*, *count/countess*. Other signifiers also can be included, for example relative size in German, where *das Haus* means *the house,* while the diminutive *das Häuschen* means *the tiny house* (there is, however, no German suffix which enlarges, so *the big house* is simply *das große Haus*).

ADJECTIVES: These are any other qualifiers closely related to the noun. Adjectives in English do not take a specific form, although there are various adjectival suffixes, e.g. *-ful* or *-ly* as in *beautiful* or *friendly*. In many languages, e.g. Spanish, adjectives need to agree with the noun in declension and gender. The order also plays an important role: *the responsible person* or *the person responsible*. The standard order of adjectives is *colour, origin, material* and *purpose: the red, French, leather riding boots*.

Qualities already included in a term's definition tend not to be added again, as doing so would produce a redundancy: *alcoholic wine, female woman*; neither are qualities contradicting its essence: *the straight curve*; nor logically false contradictory adjectives: *the black white swan*.

Adjectives in many languages are gradable and can be modified: *a very tall person, a taller person, quite a tall person, a slightly tall person, an absurdly tall person, the tallest person*. Adjectives make a language more pictoral, and convey judgements about the substances in a sentence. In Japanese the negative forms of verbs *are* adjectives, while the *beautiful* language of English uses many *clearly descriptive* adjectives, for example:

The poulterers' shops were still HALF OPEN, and the fruiterers' were RADIANT in their glory. There were GREAT, ROUND, POT-BELLIED baskets of chestnuts, SHAPED like the waistcoats of JOLLY OLD gentlemen, lolling at the doors, and tumbling out into the street in THEIR APOPLECTIC opulence. There were RUDDY, BROWN-FACED, BROAD-GIRTHED SPANISH Onions, shining in the fatness of their growth like SPANISH Friars, and winking from their shelves in WANTON slyness at the girls as they went by, and glanced demurely at the HUNG-UP mistletoe. There were pears and apples, CLUSTERED high in BLOOMING pyramids; there were bunches of grapes, made, in the shopkeepers' benevolence to dangle from CONSPICUOUS hooks, that people's mouths might water gratis as they passed; there were piles of filberts, MOSSY and BROWN, recalling, in THEIR fragrance, ANCIENT walks among the woods, and pleasant shufflings ANKLE DEEP through WITHERED leaves; there were NORFOLK Biffins, SQUAB and SWARTHY, setting off the yellow of the oranges and lemons, and, in the GREAT compactness of THEIR JUICY persons, urgently entreating and beseeching to be carried home in PAPER bags and eaten after dinner. — Charles Dickens, A Christmas Carol

ENGLISH ADJECTIVES
attributive and predicative

Adjectives describe, modify and give information about nouns and pronouns. In English, adjectives may be *attributive* or *predicative*. ATTRIBUTIVE ADJECTIVES are qualitative adjectives which are placed in front of the noun that they modify.

> A LARGE *nose is the mark of a* WITTY, COURTEOUS, AFFABLE, GENEROUS *and* LIBERAL *man.* — Cyrano de Bergerac

> *She sent for one of those* SQUAT, PLUMP LITTLE *cakes called "*PETITES *madeleines ..."* — Marcel Proust

PREDICATIVE ADJECTIVES follow such linking verbs as *be, seem, become* or *appear* and give information about the subject.

> *The roots of education are* BITTER, *but the fruit is* SWEET. — Aristotle

> *I am* INVISIBLE, *understand, simply because people refuse to see me.* — Ralph Waldo Ellison

Some adjectives can only be used attributively:

> *It is not enough to have a good mind; the* MAIN *thing is to use it well.* — Rene Descartes

while others are restricted to the predicative: We can say *"I am afraid / asleep / unwell / alive,"* but not *"I am an afraid / asleep / unwell / alive person".*

CENTRAL ADJECTIVES can be used both attributively and predicatively.

> *Every day I hear* STUPID *people say things that are not* STUPID. — Michel de Montaigne

> *The fool doth think himself* WISE, *but the* WISE *man knows himself to be a fool.* — William Shakespeare

> *There is nothing more* SILLY *than a* SILLY *laugh.* — Gaius Valerius Catulluss

QUALITATIVE ADJECTIVES can be graded to express degrees of qualities. By adding modifiers before or after a noun, we can speak of:

A FAIRLY *large nose,*
A RATHER *large nose,*
A VERY LARGE *nose,*
An EXTREMELY *large nose,*
Or *a nose that is large* ENOUGH

Adjectives can also be used to make comparisons between two or more people, things, or ideas. The three degrees of comparison are:

POSITIVE	*fair*	*happy*	*good*	*graceful*
COMPARATIVE	*fairer*	*happier*	*better*	*more graceful*
SUPERLATIVE	*fairest*	*happiest*	*best*	*most graceful*

... my love is as FAIR. *As any mother's child ...* — William Shakespeare

You shall be yet far FAIRER *than you are.* — William Shakespeare

The FAIREST *I have yet beheld.* — William Shakespeare

Adjectives can be:

QUALITATIVE — *round, jolly, outrageous, thin, crafty, powerful, dramatic*
DEMONSTRATIVE — *this, that, these, those*
DISTRIBUTIVE — *each, every, either, neither*
QUANTITATIVE — *a, some, any, no, none, little, few, many, much, 1, 2, 3 ...*
INTERROGATIVE — *which, what, whose*
POSSESSIVE — *my, your, his, her, its, our, their*
CLASSIFYING — *annual, French, chief, principal, unique, pregnant*

We are armed with language ADEQUATE *to describe each leaf of the field, but not to describe* HUMAN *character.* — Henry David Thoreau

THE VERBAL PHRASE
action!

Sentences describe action, and words which express action are called "verbs," from the Latin *verbum* "word". The VERBAL PHRASE of a sentence is a syntactic unit which involves at least one verb and its dependents e.g. *planted the tree* or *read him his last rites*. While nouns name substances, verbs are more than just names of actions—in comparison to nouns, they carry more information. Something named by a noun is comparatively static though it may have qualities and be the subject or object of an action. An action, by contrast, is far more dynamic, since it automatically invokes multiple relationships, which are examined in more detail below:

ACTION AND SUBSTANCE: There is no action without one or more substances. If I hold a bird in my hand, the action of holding requires both hand and bird, my hand is serving the action, I am subject to it, engaged with the bird. If I hold a pen, however, it may be an object in the process of my writing, even resisting it slightly. Appropriate noun declensions and verb inflections describe these subtle relationships.

ACTION AND AGENT: For every action there is a reason. Today, we commonly distinguish between conscious and unconscious agents: If *I hold a sword*, I have probably made a conscious decision to do so, while if *the wind blows*, there may or may not be a being originating the action. When the agent is uncertain, we can use constructions such as *it rains*, but the agent of an action is not necessarily the prime cause for the action: If *I smell the flower*, I might have done nothing but expose my nose to its scent. Our sentences express our experience of cause and effect, and verbs do this through *active* and *passive voices*, e.g. *The sun shines / I am exposed to sunlight*.

ACTION AND PERSON: As we speak, we are already committing an act; a speech-act. Whatever we say relates to ourselves, so I may refer to actions involving myself, involving whomever I am speaking to, or involving others. In English, the categories of *first*, *second* and *third* person *singular* (*I, thee, he/she/it*), and *plural* (*We, ye, they*) denote person. In heavily-inflected languages such as Polish, however, verbs have different endings for *I, You, He, She, It, We both, We all, You both, You all, They both, They all*, etc.

ACTION AND TIME: While substance is eternal, action is change, and change happens in time. Any action can therefore either have already happened, be happening, or happen in the future: *past*, *present* and *future tense*. The position in time of the action is the *tense* of the verb.

ACTION AND ASPECT: The aspect of a verb describes whether the action is simple, ongoing, has been completed, or will be completed in the future, e.g. *I sing, I am singing*. In some languages, aspects can also describe actions as being repetitive, successful, defective, resumptive or accidental (*see appendix, page 58*). In Slavic languages, aspect counts more heavily than either tense or mood, conveyed via prefixes and suffixes to the verb.

ACTION AND MOOD: Actions can really be taking place, or be only proposed, stated, or hypothetical in other ways. These are the moods of a verb; compare *I insist I am involved* to *I insist I be involved*.

VERBS & TIME
it's still doing it

Substances change over time, and so do their relation to one another, and the changes substances suffer or cause in time are called *actions*. Thus verbs, by naming actions, carry information about time in the verb's MODE or TENSE, relative to the moment when the speech takes place. Different languages describe time differently via different modes. In the Navajo language, for example, seven verb modes distinguish between the IMPERFECTIVE, *I am in the act of walking*, the PERFECTIVE, *I walked*, the PROGRESSIVE, *I am walking*, the FUTURE, *I shall walk*, the USITATIVE, *I usually walk*, the ITERATIVE, *I always walk*, and the OPTATIVE, *I hope I walk*.

The ancient Greek language used two distinct words for time, *chronos* for a stretch of time and *kairos* for a moment in time. These qualities of time are described by a verb's ASPECT, e.g. the lion *catches the mouse* or *is catching the mouse*. In some languages, e.g. Chinese, neither tense nor aspect is differentiated, while in Navajo again, there are twelve possible aspects with ten subaspects (*see appendix of verb aspects, page 58*).

English, and all other Indo-European languages, make a clear distinction in tense between *past, present, and future*, and the verb's aspect additionally colours the action as being either perfected, *the lion has caught the mouse*, or not yet perfected, *the lion is catching the mouse*. Verbs also can be modulated in other ways, e.g. the passive voice, *the mouse is caught by the lion*. These verb forms can be drawn in a grid (*e.g. see opposite*), where the location in the grid conveys specific information. Verb tenses thus allow narration to be logically structured in time. A sentence such as *yesterday I will go to school* becomes grammatical nonsense, since the verb form and the temporal adjective are in contradiction.

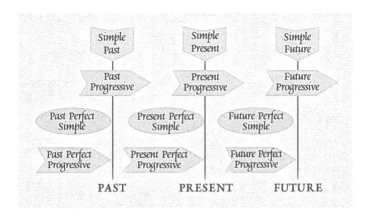

Further nuances to actions are provided by adverbs. In English many adjectives take adverbial forms by adding *-ly*, *he slowly walks*, though some words ending with *-ly* are adjectives, e.g. *a friendly smile*. Adverbs, like adjectives, can be modified by other adverbs such as *quite*, *very*, *mildly*, *extremely* in order to add further clarification.

Verbs in many languages change their form quite radically in accordance with the subject of the sentence and their time reference; this process is called the CONJUGATION of the verb. Compare, for example: *am*, *are*, *is*, *was*, all of which are conjugated forms of *to be*. Older verbs tend to retain their strong (or irregular) conjugation, but most English verbs show very little inflection, e.g. *I laugh*, *he laughs*.

The most basic form of a verb is called the INFINITIVE. In English, the infinitive consists of the marker *to* and the BASE FORM, so that *to be* is the infinitive form of that verb. Subsequently, when speaking about a verb, it is generally named in that form, and we thus refer to the verb *to be* rather than to the word *are*, which is considered a form of *to be*.

ENGLISH VERB TENSES
about time too

The TENSE of a verb refers to the location in time of an action or event.

The PRESENT TENSE is used to indicate something that is happening or existing now, is a recurring event, or is true at all times.

> *But soft! What light through yonder window BREAKS?*
> *It is the East, and Juliet IS the sun!* — William Shakespeare

> *Every time a child SAYS "I don't believe in fairies" there is*
> *a little fairy somewhere that falls down dead.* — James M. Barrie

> *He who OPENS a school door, CLOSES a prison.* — Victor Hugo

> *Don't grieve. Anything you lose COMES round in another form.* — Jalaluddin Rumi

The PAST TENSE indicates that something happened or existed in the past.

> *The world's bright candle, early Spring, CAME new*
> *   And BROUGHT the bounteous gift of life restored,*
> *And SPREAD afar its veil of pearly blue,*
> *   And URGED the nightingale to trill its song;*
> *SPREAD far the limped wine of morning dew,*
> *   And FILLED the open'd tulip's crimson cup;*
> *INFLAMED the rose that in the garden BLEW*
> *   Agleam with turquoise and the ruby's glow.*
>
> Muhammed Fuzuli (translated by Sofi Nuri)

Unlike most other languages, English does not have inflected forms for the FUTURE TENSE. *Future time* can be expressed in a variety of ways:

This suspense is terrible. I hope it WILL LAST. — Oscar Wilde

By putting forward the hands of the clock
you SHALL NOT ADVANCE the hour. — Victor Hugo

You have to have an idea of what you ARE GOING TO DO,
but it should be a vague idea. — Pablo Picasso

Tomorrow, every Fault IS TO BE AMENDED;
but that Tomorrow never comes. — Benjamin Franklin

I have always imagined that Paradise WILL BE some kind of library. — Jorge
Luis Borges

The possible TENSES of a verb, combined with its possible ASPECTS, create a grid of distinct possibilities:

	TENSE		
	PAST	PRESENT	FUTURE
ASPECT			
SIMPLE	*he spoke*	*he speaks*	*he will speak*
PROGRESSIVE	*he was speaking*	*he is speaking*	*he will be speaking*
PERFECT	*he had spoken*	*he has spoken*	*he will have spoken*

ENGLISH VERB FORMS
the five forms

All VERBS inflect, or change their form, to express changes in tense, person, number and voice. The majority of verbs in the English language are regular verbs and follow a set pattern of five forms:

BASE INFINITIVE TO	PRESENT TENSE -S	SIMPLE PAST -ED	PRESENT PARTICIPLE -ING	PAST PARTICIPLE HAVE -ED
to walk	walk / walks	walked	walking	have / has / had walked
to dream	dream / dreams	dreamed	dreaming	have / has / had dreamed
to dance	dance / dances	danced	dancing	have / has / had danced

IRREGULAR VERBS also have five forms, but follow different patterns:

to be	am / is / are	was / were	being	been
to have	have / has	had	having	had
to do	do / does	did	doing	did
to go	go / goes	went	going	gone
to eat	eat / eats	ate	eating	eaten
to speak	speak / speaks	spoke	speaking	spoken

Finite TO FAIL, but infinite TO VENTURE. — Emily Dickinson

There are two key classes of verb: MAIN VERBS (also known as LEXICAL VERBS) and AUXILIARY VERBS. MAIN VERBS express the meaning of a clause. They show action, possession or states of being.

> I THINK *therefore* I AM. — René Descartes

AUXILIARY VERBS add information to the main verb in order to refer to actual events or situations in the past or the present. The primary auxiliaries are *be, have* and *do* (and their corresponding conjugated forms).

> *Happy he who, like Ulysses,* HAS COMPLETED *a great journey.* — Du Bellay les Regrets

> *I was angry with my friend: I told my wrath, my wrath* DID END.
> *I was angry with my foe: I told it not, my wrath* DID GROW. — William Blake

> *In the world through which I travel,*
> I AM *endlessly* CREATING *myself.* — Frantz Fanon

The primary auxiliaries also can stand alone as the main verb of a clause.

> *"I* HAVE *no name /* I AM *but two days old". / What shall I call thee?*
> *"I happy* AM, *Joy* IS *my name". / Sweet joy befall thee!* — William Blake

> *Nature* DOES *nothing uselessly.* — Aristotle

MODAL AUXILIARY VERBS help the main verb to express a range of meanings, including possibility, probability, desirability, permission, requests, suggestions, instructions, wants, wishes, obligations and necessity; *will, would, shall, should, may, might, can, could, must, ought (to).*

> *Men* WOULD *live exceedingly quiet if these*
> *two words, mine and thine were taken away.* — Anaxagoras

> *We* SHOULD *come home from adventures, and perils,*
> *and discoveries every day with new experience and character.* — Henry David Thoreau

> *Like weather, men's fortune* MAY *change by the evening.* — Luu Mengsheng

TO BE

or not

INFINITIVE			to be	
		PRESENT		PAST
SINGULAR	I	am		was
	you	are		were
	he/she/it	is		was
PLURAL	we	are		were
	you	are		were
	they	are		were
PARTICIPLE			being	

The verb TO BE describes a state, rather than an action, and takes very irregular forms in accordance with the subject of the sentence. As we all know, existence is a complicated affair!

To be can be used as a main verb: *There is something in the cupboard.* Here *to be* functions as a copula in that it connects terms expressing identity, location, class membership, or predication (among other things): *One and one is two; stars are celestial objects; the house is big enough; this is true.* When used with another verb in the infinitive, *to be* can also express obligation or fate: *He is to be executed.*

However, the most frequent use of *to be*, in English as well as in many other Western European languages, is as an auxiliary verb in various cases including continuous forms and the passive voice, such as: *I am going; we were running; the city was destroyed.*

People have been contemplating the essence of *to be* for thousands of years, and the connection it suggests between action and existence.

TO HAVE
do have a go

		PRESENT	PAST
INFINITIVE		*to have*	
SINGULAR	I	have	had
	you	*have*	*had*
	he/she/it	has	*had*
PLURAL	we	*have*	*had*
	you	*have*	*had*
	they	*have*	*had*
PARTICIPLE		*having*	

The irregular verb TO HAVE also often serves as an auxiliary: *If she had noticed the mistake, she would have corrected it.* As a main verb, it has various meanings: In *I have a cold,* it describes a state of being; in *I have to go*, it denotes obligation; in *I have a car*, it expresses possession or belonging, like the possessive form of a noun or pronoun (the GENITIVE *'s*): *my father's car, his car.* It can also express obligation via the infinitive: *You have to bow;* or the participle: *I am having this fixed.* English uses *to have* to form the perfect aspect: *I have pondered.*

Other irregular verbs also have special roles. *To do* can stand in for an action previously referred to much like a pronoun stands for a noun we already know about: *I love swimming; So do I.* Sometimes it can appear as a main *and* auxiliary verb: *How do you do?* *To go* also has a special role. Since English lacks a specific form for the future tense, it instead uses *to go* and modal verbs such as *will* and *shall* to suggest the future: *I am going to swim; they are going to miss the boat.*

VERB VOICE
active and passive

The ACTIVE VOICE and PASSIVE VOICE express whether the action is being done or received by the subject. The two voices may occur in any tense.

ACTIVE

> How could youths better LEARN to live than by at once
> trying the experiment of living? — Henry David Thoreau

> The things which I HAVE SEEN I now can SEE no more. — William Wordsworth

> It was high counsel that I once HEARD given to a young person,
> "always do what you are afraid to do". — Ralph Waldo Emerson

PASSIVE

> A man's character MAY BE LEARNED from the adjectives
> which he habitually uses in conversation. — Mark Twain

> I am the one, whose art WAS SEEN by the blind,
> and whose words WERE HEARD by the deaf. — Al Mutannabi

VERB ASPECT
simple, progressive and perfect

A verb's ASPECT tells us whether the status in time of an action or state, whether it is indefinite, has been completed, or is still in progress. The SIMPLE ASPECT merely indicates an action.

> What you SEEK is seeking you. — Jalaluddin Rumi

The PROGRESSIVE ASPECT indicates continuing action in the past, present, or future.

> While I thought THAT I WAS LEARNING how to live,
> I have been learning how to die. — Leonardo da Vinci

> We have watered the trees that blossom in the summer-time. Now let's
> sprinkle those whose flowering time is past. That will be the better deed,
> because WE SHALL NOT BE WORKING for the reward. — Kalidasa

The PERFECT ASPECT indicates that an action has been completed, or will be completed at some point in the future.

> I know many books which HAVE BORED their readers,
> but I know of none which has done real evil. — Voltaire

> All the fruit will be off the Christmas tree then; the crackers WILL HAVE CRACKED
> OFF; the almonds WILL HAVE BEEN CRUNCHED; and the sweet-bitter riddles
> WILL HAVE BEEN READ; the lights will have perished off the dark green boughs;
> the toys growing on them WILL HAVE BEEN DISTRIBUTED, FOUGHT FOR,
> CHERISHED, NEGLECTED, BROKEN. — William Makepeace Thackeray

The PERFECT and PROGRESSIVE ASPECTS can be combined.

> Hetty HAD BEEN DECEIVING herself in thinking that she could love and
> marry him: SHE HAD BEEN LOVING Arthur all the while: and now, in her
> desperation at the nearness of their marriage, she had run away. — George Eliot

VERB MOOD
a manner of speaking

The MOOD of a verb expresses the conditions under which an action or condition is taking place. It refers to the attitude or manner of the person who is speaking or writing. In English there are three moods.

The INDICATIVE MOOD is used to express fact or opinion.

> Love IS a serious mental disease. — Plato

> Behind every successful man STANDS a surprised mother-in-law. — Voltaire

The IMPERATIVE MOOD is used to give orders, commands, directives, or to make requests.

> LIVE your life, DO your work, then TAKE your hat. — Henry David Thoreau

> Friends, Romans, countrymen, LEND me your ears. — William Shakespeare

> DON'T COUNT your chickens before they are hatched. — Aesop

The SUBJUNCTIVE MOOD expresses wishes, commands, desires, possibility, necessity, and hypothetical supposition.

> I would my horse HAD the speed of your tongue. — William Shakespeare

> Suppose you WERE an idiot and suppose you WERE a member of Congress. But I repeat myself. — Mark Twain

> We would often be sorry if our wishes WERE granted. — Aesop

The FORMULAIC SUBJUNCTIVE uses set formulas.

> BE that as it may; far BE it from me; PERISH the thought; SUFFICE it to say; if it PLEASE the court; truth BE told; Long LIVE the Queen; God BLESS you.

COMPLEX VERB PHRASES
processions of verbs

The two tenses (present and past) and four aspects of the English language combine using auxiliaries to create a matrix of verb forms. Up to five positions may be identified in a verb phrase. The modal verb comes first (*might, could, should, would*), the main verb last, and between them up to three auxiliary verbs may specify aspect and tense. The table below shows a scheme of complex English verb phrases including modal verbs.

	1	2	3	4	5
It	might				explode
She		has			vanished
They			were		singing
He		had	been		skating
It	might	have		been	dropped
We	may	have	been	being	followed
TYPE	modal v.	perfect aux.	progr. aux.	passive aux.	main verb
MAIN VERB	base form	-ed participle	-ing part.	-ed part.	
MEANING	modalised	perfect aspect	progr. asp.	is passive	

In a similar fashion, for its future tenses, English uses either the present tense with a future time phrase, or modals, e.g. *we are leaving tomorrow*, or *I will/shall leave tomorrow*. The same technique also provides constructions for further tenses such as the FUTURE PERFECT, *I will have left by tomorrow*, and the FUTURE PROGRESSIVE, *he will be waiting*.

NEGATIVES
don't won't can't

In English, auxiliary and modal verbs are required to form NEGATIVE SENTENCES: *I do not believe that* rather than *I believe that not.* There is no direct negation of main verbs in modern prose English, instead the word *not* can only appear after auxiliaries or modals: *I go—I am not going; I swim—I do not swim; I will help—I will not help.*

There are, however, two cases in which negation does not adhere to this rule. One is with the main verb *hope*, which is not negated with the auxiliary *do*: *I hope he wins—I hope not.* The other is the modal *must*: *You must go* is negated as *you don't have to go* rather than as *you must not go.*

The negations of auxiliary and modal words often have CONTRACTED FORMS, and although these are common in spoken English, they are frowned upon in writing: *can + not = cannot* or *can't; do + not = don't, will + not = won't; have + not = haven't.*

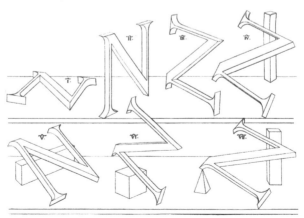

VERB TRANSITIVITY
to take or not to take

TRANSITIVE VERBS require an object to complete their meaning.

> You can CUT all the flowers but you cannot KEEP spring from coming. — Pablo Neruda

> By putting forward the hands of the clock
> you shall not ADVANCE the hour. — Victor Hugo

INTRANSITIVE VERBS do not require an object, but may be accompanied by an adverbial word or phrase.

> Some RISE by sin, and some by virtue FALL. — William Shakespeare

> A man KNOWS when he is growing old because
> he BEGINS to look like his father. — Gabriel Garcia Marquez

Some verbs can be used *transitively* or *intransitively*.

> The sun, with all those planets revolving around it and dependent on it, can still RIPEN a bunch of grapes as if it had nothing else in the universe to do. — Galileo Galilei

> The wise man does not grow old, but RIPENS. — Victor Hugo

DITRANSITIVE VERBS take a *direct object* and an *indirect object* at the same time.

> GIVE every man thy ear, but few thy voice. — William Shakespeare

> By plucking her petals, you do not GATHER
> the beauty of the flower. — Rabindranath Tagore

FINITE & COPULAR VERBS
alone or linking

A FINITE VERB has a subject and shows tense and number. It can stand by itself as the main verb of a sentence.

> Hope IS the thing with feathers / That PERCHES in the soul
> And SINGS the tune without the words / And never STOPS at all. — Emily Dickinson

> If a thing LOVES, it IS infinite. — William Blake

A NON-FINITE VERB (VERBAL) cannot stand alone as a main verb of a sentence. The non-finite verb forms are: the *infinitive*, and the *present* and *past participles*.

> Clouds come FLOATING into my life, no longer TO CARRY rain or USHER storm, but TO ADD colour to my sunset sky. — Rabindranath Tagore

> DANCING begets warmth, which is the parent of wantonness. — Henry Fielding

> Of all the noises KNOWN to man, opera is the most expensive. — Molière

> Everything CONSIDERED, work is less boring than amusing oneself. — Baudelaire

COPULAR VERBS are linking verbs such as be, seem, appear, feel, remain, become, smell and look which join a subject to its complement.

> When a thought takes one's breath away,
> a grammar lesson SEEMS an impertinence. — Thomas W. Higginson

> My pen IS my harp and my lyre;
> my library IS my garden and my orchard. — Judah Ha-Levi

IS IT A VERB?
confusion in class

Words can belong to more than one class, depending on the role that they play in a sentence. For example, some words can be either a NOUN or a VERB.

> How can we know the dancer from the DANCE? — William Butler Yeats

> Let us read and let us DANCE—two amusements
> that will never do any harm to the world. — Voltaire

NOUNS or ADJECTIVES.

> Happiness resides not in possessions and not in GOLD,
> happiness dwells in the soul. — Democritus

> Rich and rare were the gems she wore,
> And a bright GOLD ring on her hand she bore. — Thomas Moore

A word can function as an ADVERB, a PREPOSITION, or a CONJUNCTION.

> A great part of courage is the courage of having
> done the thing BEFORE. — Ralph Waldo Emerson

> A dreamer is one who can only find his way by moonlight, and his punishment
> is that he sees the dawn BEFORE the rest of the world. — Oscar Wilde

> The woods are lovely, dark and deep. But I have promises
> to keep, and miles to go BEFORE I sleep. — Robert Frost

Or even fulfil the functions of ADVERB, ADJECTIVE, NOUN, or VERB.

> Ever tried. Ever failed. No matter.
> Try Again. Fail again. Fail BETTER. — Samuel Beckett

> He does it with BETTER grace, but I do it more natural. — William Shakespeare

ADVERBS
elaborating on the action

ADVERBS are used to modify verbs, adjectives or other adverbs. They provide information about:

TIME – *now, immediately, yesterday*

PLACE – *there, here, anywhere, nowhere, hither, yon, thence, thither, upstairs*

MANNER – *happily, carefully, disdainfully*

REASON AND PURPOSE – *consequently, so, because*

FREQUENCY – *always, seldom, never*

DEGREE – *very, extremely, more, less*

DURATION – *forever*

A true friend unbosoms FREELY, *advises* JUSTLY, *assists* READILY, *adventures* BOLDLY, *takes all* PATIENTLY, *defends* COURAGEOUSLY, *and continues a friend* UNCHANGEABLY. — William Penn

It's NEVER *the wrong time to call on Toad.* EARLY *or* LATE *he's* ALWAYS *the same fellow.* ALWAYS *good-tempered,* ALWAYS *glad to see you,* ALWAYS *sorry when you go!* — Kenneth Grahame

SLOWLY, SLOWLY *O mind, everything in own pace happens. The gardener may water a hundred buckets, fruit arrives* ONLY *in its season* — Kabir

He was a fiddler, and CONSEQUENTLY *a rogue.* — Jonathan Swift

The intelligent man finds almost everything ridiculous, the sensible man HARDLY *anything.* — J. W. von Goethe

The good ended HAPPILY, *and the bad* UNHAPPILY. *That is what fiction means.* — Oscar Wilde

Poets have been MYSTERIOUSLY *silent on the subject of cheese.* — G. K. Chesterton

CONJUNCTIVE ADVERBS link two clauses; *moreover, however, accordingly, otherwise, undoubtedly*

> Lies are essential to humanity. They are perhaps as important as the pursuit of pleasure and MOREOVER are dictated by that pursuit. — Marcel Proust

INTERROGATIVE ADVERBS ask: *why, where, how, when*

> HOW shall a man escape from that which is written;
> HOW shall he flee from his destiny? — Ferdowsi

> WHY should we be in such desperate haste to succeed, and in such desperate enterprises? If a man does not keep pace with his companions, perhaps it is because he hears a different drummer. — Henry David Thoreau

Adverbs can be used to emphasise, amplify, or tone down adjectives or other adverbs.

> History books that contain no lies are EXTREMELY dull. — Anatole France

> I like my body when it is with your body. It is SO QUITE new a thing. Muscles better and nerves more. — E. E. Cummings

Adverbs are usually optional, and can be removed without affecting grammatical structure or meaning.

> And what he (GREATLY) thought, he (NOBLY) dared. — Homer

Most adverbs can be placed at the beginning, middle or end of a sentence.

> SOMETIMES small things lead to great joys. — Shmuel Agnon

> It is in our idleness, in our dreams, that the submerged truth SOMETIMES comes to the top. — Virginia Woolf

> 'Tis healthy to be sick SOMETIMES. — Henry David Thoreau

LITTLE WORDS
conjunctions, prepositions, etc.

Since English, like Chinese, uses so little inflection to express relations between its terms, it instead relies heavily on *form words* or *copula* to express these relations. An average page of written English has a huge number of little words, mostly conjunctions and prepositions, compared to one written in a heavily inflected language like Sanskrit or Polish.

While nouns, verbs, adjectives and adverbs are open classes, with new words entering the vocabulary on a daily basis, these form words are what we call a closed class, so can be listed in their entirety. Again, we are stumbling on a philosophical question: are these all the possible relations between substances and actions, or are there further relations, which we only have difficulty imagining due to a lack of words?

Little words have been compared to seeds. It is possible that the original primitive language of our ancestors comprised of a small collection of simple sounds, the smallest building blocks of meaning. Then, like atoms combining to make molecules, these sounds, or *morphemes*, combined into words. Finally, as time passed and pronounciations changed, we lost knowledge of exactly what these building blocks were.

CONJUNCTIONS
joining together

CONJUNCTIONS join words, phrases or clauses together and show the relationship between them. COORDINATING CONJUNCTIONS join two items (words, phrases or clauses) of equal grammatical status: *for, and, nor, but, or, yet, so.*

> *The rose AND the thorn, AND sorrow AND gladness are linked together.* — Saadi

CORRELATIVE CONJUNCTIONS always appear in pairs and are used to link equivalent sentence elements: *both…and, either…or, neither…nor, not only …but also, so…as, whether…or.*

> It is NOT ONLY what we do, BUT ALSO what
> we do not do for which we are accountable. — Molière

SUBORDINATING CONJUNCTIONS link two items of unequal grammatical status and indicate the nature of the relationship among the independent clause(s) and the dependent clause(s):

after, as, as if, as long as, as much as, as soon as, as though, because, before, by the time, even if, even though, if, in order that, in case, lest

once, only if, provided that, since, so that, than, that, though, till, unless, until, when, whenever, where, wherever, while

> Some cause happiness WHEREVER they go;
> others WHENEVER they go. — Oscar Wilde

> AS LONG AS a word remains unspoken, you are its master;
> ONCE you utter it, you are its slave. — Solomon Ibn Gabirol

PREPOSITIONS
tiny relationships

PREPOSITIONS are used to link two parts of a clause or sentence, and show a relationship in space, time, cause, manner or means.

> PREPOSITIONS OF SPATIAL LOCATION: *at (point), on (surface), in (volume).*

> PREPOSITIONS OF SPATIAL DIRECTION: *to, onto, into, through, out of, towards, away from, up, down, around.*

> PREPOSITIONS OF SPATIAL RELATIONSHIP: *by, off, along, across, against, among, beside, near, next to, between, among, ahead of, in front of, in the middle of, inside, round, opposite, behind, from, beyond, off, within, over, on top of, above, below, beneath, under, underneath, following.*

> PREPOSITIONS OF TIME: *on, at, in, after, before, since, for, by, from, until, during, within, throughout.*

> PREPOSITIONS OF CAUSE, MANNER AND MEANS: *as, of, about, but, despite, except, than, with, without, minus, plus, like, unlike, via, because of, apart from, along with, as for, instead of, up to, in case of, according to.*

He said the pleasantest manner OF spending a hot July day was lying FROM morning TILL evening ON a bank OF heath IN the middle OF the moors, WITH the bees humming dreamily ABOUT AMONG the bloom, and the larks singing high UP OVERHEAD, and the blue sky and bright sun shining steadily and cloudlessly. — Emily Brontë

46

SUBJECT & PREDICATE
a little logic

We are now in a position to begin putting together the various elements of our little book. Every complete SENTENCE consists of a SUBJECT, which performs the action of a verb, and a PREDICATE which modifies the subject. The SUBJECT comes at or near the beginning of a clause, and precedes the verb. A SIMPLE SUBJECT can be a noun or pronoun.

> MOONLIGHT *is sculpture.* — Nathaniel Hawthorne

> HE *was happily married—but his wife wasn't.* — Victor Borge

A COMPLETE SUBJECT can be a noun phrase or clause, and includes the noun or pronoun, plus any modifiers.

> *Have patience.* ALL THINGS *are difficult before they become easy.* — Saadi

> THE MAN WHO DOES NOT READ GOOD BOOKS *has no advantage over the man who cannot read them.* — Mark Twain

The SIMPLE PREDICATE consists of the main verb and any auxiliary verbs.

> *The flower that smells the sweetest* IS *shy and lowly.* — William Wordsworth

> *A mule* WILL LABOR *ten years willingly and patiently for you, for the privilege of kicking you once.* — William Faulkner

The COMPLETE PREDICATE includes the verb, along with any direct or indirect objects, complements, and adverbials.

> *All the ills of mankind, all the tragic misfortunes that fill the history books, all the political blunders, all the failures of the great leaders,* HAVE ARISEN MERELY FROM A LACK OF SKILL AT DANCING. — Molière

THE FIVE PHRASES
putting it all together

A PHRASE is a word, or a small group of related words, that functions as a grammatical unit. In English grammar, we distinguish five types of phrase which take their names from their central element, or *head word*. In addition to the head word, phrases may have pre- and post-head strings composed of determiners, modifiers, objects or complements.

A NOUN PHRASE, as we have already seen, consists of a noun or a pronoun head-word, and any determiners and modifiers.

> THE INSUFFERABLE ARROGANCE OF HUMAN BEINGS *to think that Nature was made solely for their benefit, as if it was conceivable that the sun had been set afire merely to ripen* MEN'S APPLES *and head* THEIR CABBAGES.
> — Cyrano de Bergerac

VERB PHRASES are composed of a verb head word, which may be preceded by a *negative* word such as *not* or *never*, as well as any auxiliaries.

> *Whenever you* ARGUE *with another wiser than yourself in order that others* MAY ADMIRE *your wisdom, they* WILL DISCOVER *your ignorance.* — Saadi

> *You* MIGHT, *from your appearance,* BE *the wife of Lucifer. Nevertheless,* YOU SHALL NOT GET *the better of me. I* AM *an Englishwoman.* — Charles Dickens

The ADJECTIVE PHRASE has an adjective as the head word, and may include an adverb or adverb phrase as the pre-head string.

> *The person, be it gentleman or lady, who has not pleasure in a* GOOD *novel, must be* INTOLERABLY STUPID. — Jane Austen

> *It is a* VERY SAD *thing that nowadays there is* SO LITTLE USELESS *information.* — Oscar Wilde

> I really do not know that anything has ever been MORE EXCITING than diagramming sentences. — Gertrude Stein

ADVERB PHRASES have an adverb as the *head word*, with modifiers before, after or both.

> Who you are speaks SO LOUDLY I can't hear what you're saying. — Ralph Waldo Emerson

> The universe is full of magical things, PATIENTLY waiting for our wits to grow sharper. — Eden Phillpotts

A PREPOSITIONAL PHRASE consists of a preposition, a noun or pronoun that serves as its complement, and any modifiers.

> A Christmas frost had come AT MIDSUMMER; a white December storm had whirled OVER JUNE; ice glazed the ripe apples, drifts crushed the blowing roses; ON HAYFIELD AND CORNFIELD lay a frozen shroud: lanes which last night blushed full of flowers, to-day were pathless WITH UNTRODDEN SNOW and the woods, which twelve hours since waved leafy and flagrant as groves BETWEEN THE TROPICS, now spread, waste, wild, and white as pine-forests IN WINTRY NORWAY. — Charlotte Brontë

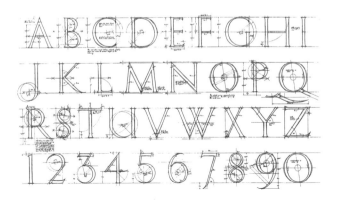

CLAUSES
elements

A CLAUSE is a sentence or sentence-like construction. In the English language, there are seven clause elements:

Subject (s)   *Direct Object* (DO)   *Subject Complement* (SC)   *Adverbial* (A)
Verb (V)   *Indirect Object* (IO)   *Object Complement* (OC)

The SUBJECT gives the clause its theme, or topic, and may be a noun, a noun phrase, a participial form, or another clause. The subject performs the action of a verb.

> LIFE *shrinks or expands in proportion to one's courage.* — Anais Nin

> A MAN'S HOMELAND *is wherever he prospers.* — Aristophanes

> WHAT I LIKE TO DRINK MOST *is wine that belongs to others.* — Diogenes

The VERB indicates the occurrence or performance of an action, or the existence of a state or condition. The verb must agree with the subject in person and number.

> *Whatever you* CAN DO, *or* DREAM *you* CAN, BEGIN *it. Boldness* HAS *genius, power, and magic in it.* BEGIN *it now.* — J. W. von Goethe

A DIRECT OBJECT directly receives the action of or is affected by the verb. Like the subject, the object of a clause can be a noun, pronoun, noun phrase, present participle or another clause.

> *Every day we should hear at least* ONE LITTLE SONG, *read* ONE GOOD POEM, *see* ONE EXQUISITE PICTURE, *and, if possible, speak* A FEW SENSIBLE WORDS. — J. W. von Goethe

An INDIRECT OBJECT receives the action of or benefits from the direct object.

If you want to annoy your neighbours, tell the truth about THEM. — Pietro Aretino

A COMPLEMENT is a word, phrase or clause which is necessary to complete the meaning of a word. A SUBJECT COMPLEMENT follows a copular (linking) verb and completes the meaning of the subject.

Friendship is THE SHADOW OF THE EVENING, *which increases with the setting sun of life.* — Jean De La Fontaine

A book is A GARDEN, AN ORCHARD, A STOREHOUSE, A PARTY, A COMPANY BY THE WAY, A COUNSELLOR, A MULTITUDE OF COUNSELLORS. — Charles Baudelaire

The OBJECT COMPLEMENT is a noun, noun phrase, adjective, or adjective phrase that modifies or refers to the direct object.

I do not say a proverb is amiss when aptly and reasonably applied, but to be forever discharging them, right or wrong, hit or miss, renders conversation INSIPID AND VULGAR. — Miguel de Cervantes

A ruffled mind makes A RESTLESS PILLOW. — Charlotte Brontë

ADVERBIALS provide more information about a clause and can be an *adverb, adverb phrase, prepositional* and *noun phrase*, as well as a *subordinate clause.* A clause may contain more than one adverbial.

Do not train a child TO LEARN BY FORCE OR HARSHNESS; *but direct them* TO IT BY WHAT AMUSES THEIR MINDS, *so that you may be* BETTER ABLE TO DISCOVER WITH ACCURACY *the peculiar bent* OF THE GENIUS OF EACH. — Plato

Not every clause needs an adverbial, but some verbs are grammatically incomplete without one.

Aspects are WITHIN US, *and who seems* MOST KINGLY *is king.* — Thomas Hardy

Words mean MORE THAN WHAT IS SET DOWN ON PAPER. *It takes the human voice* TO INFUSE THEM WITH DEEPER MEANING. — Maya Angelou

TYPES OF CLAUSE
in a nutshell

An INDEPENDENT CLAUSE is a simple sentence that can stand alone.

> *The creation of a thousand forests is in one acorn.* — Ralph Waldo Emerson

> *The greater part of the world's troubles are due to questions and grammar.*
> — Michel de Montaigne

A COORDINATE CLAUSE is a clause linked to another clause by a COORDINATING CONJUNCTION: *and, but, nor, or, then, yet.*

> *A mother's arms are made of tenderness* AND CHILDREN SLEEP SOUNDLY IN THEM. — Victor Hugo

> *If you do not expect the unexpected you will not find it,* FOR IT IS NOT TO BE REACHED BY SEARCH OR TRAIL. — Heraclitus

A SUBORDINATE or DEPENDENT CLAUSE is linked to a main clause by a *subordinating conjunction.* When one clause complements another clause, it is subordinate to it. There are subordinating conjunctions of:

Time — *after, before, as soon as, since, when, whenever, while*

> *All men* WHILST THEY ARE AWAKE *are in one common world: but each of them,* WHEN HE IS ASLEEP, *is in a world of his own.* — Plutarch

> WHEN I GET A LITTLE MONEY, *I buy books.*
> *And if there is any left over, I buy food.* — Desiderius Erasmus

Concession — *al/though, even though, despite, except that, much as, not that, whereas, while/whilst*

> *It is the part of a gallant man to say nothing,* THOUGH HE MAY INDICATE *that he could say a great deal.* — Sir Arthur Conan Doyle

Condition — *if, provided that, as long as, unless*

"IF YOU LIVED ON CABBAGE, *you would not be obliged to flatter the powerful*". To which the courtier replied, "IF YOU FLATTERED THE POWERFUL, *you would not be obliged to live upon cabbage*".
— Diogenes, *Advice to a Young Courtier*

Reason — *because, since, as*

A bird doesn't sing BECAUSE IT HAS AN ANSWER, *it sings* BECAUSE IT HAS A SONG. — Maya Angelou

Result — *so, thus*

I love you without knowing how, or when, or from where.
I love you straightforwardly, without complexities or pride;
SO I LOVE YOU BECAUSE I KNOW NO OTHER WAY. — Pablo Neruda

Comparison — *than, as*

Better by far you should forget and smile THAN THAT YOU SHOULD REMEMBER AND BE SAD. — Christina G. Rossetti

A clause can be FINITE or NON-FINITE, according to the type of verb it contains.

A RELATIVE CLAUSE is a dependent clause generally introduced by a *relative pronoun* such as *who, whom, that, which, whose, when, where.*

I would venture to guess that Anon, WHO WROTE SO MANY POEMS WITHOUT SIGNING THEM, *was often a woman.* — Virginia Woolf

The REDUCED RELATIVE CLAUSE, has no relative pronoun, and the verb is non-finite.

But words are things, and a small drop of ink,
FALLING LIKE DEW, *upon a thought, produces*
That which makes thousands, perhaps millions, think. — George Gordon Byron

SENTENCES
putting it all together

The SENTENCE is the largest unit of grammar. It is often defined as the expression of a complete thought, although one person's complete thought may not be another's. Perhaps the simplest way to define sentence is to say that it is a meaningful string of words with a capital letter at the beginning, and a stop of some kind at the end.

> Oh Romeo! Romeo! Wherefore art though Romeo?
>> Deny thy father and refuse thy name:
> Or if thou wilt not, be but sworn my love
>> And I'll no longer be a Capulet. — William Shakespeare

There are four different types of sentences:

EXCLAMATORY SENTENCES express strong feelings or emotion:

> Oh Romeo! Romeo!

INTERROGATIVE SENTENCES are used to request information or ask questions:

> Wherefore art thou Romeo?

IMPERATIVE SENTENCES request action, give directives or commands (understood subject):

> Deny thy father and refuse thy name.

DECLARATIVE SENTENCES make statements, convey information:

> I'll no longer be a Capulet.

The SIMPLE sentence has a single verb phrase and is made up of one independent clause:

> Necessity has the face of a dog. — Gabriel García Márquez

> *Brevity is the soul of wit.* — William Shakespeare

COMPOUND sentences contain two or more independent clauses, which may be linked by coordination, by a conjunct, or by a comma or semi-colon.

> *She might have beguiled the loneliness of her days with old songs and poems, but she really did not have much feeling for such things.* — Murasaki Shikibu (trans. G. Seidensticker)

> *Age considers; youth ventures.* — Rabindranath Tagore

A COMPLEX sentence consists of one main clause and at least one subordinate clause.

> *When we remember we are all mad, the mysteries disappear and life stands explained.* — Mark Twain

> *How did it happen that their lips came together? How does it happen that birds sing, that snow melts, that the rose unfolds, that the dawn whitens behind the stark shapes of trees on the quivering summit of the hill? A kiss, and all was said.* — Victor Hugo

COMPOUND-COMPLEX is a compound sentence with more than one main clause and at least one subordinate clause.

> *We are not satisfied with real life; we want to live some imaginary life in the eyes of other people and to seem different from what we actually are.* — Blaise Pascal

> *What is life? A madness. What is life? An illusion, a shadow, a story. And the greatest good is little enough; for all life is a dream, and dreams themselves are only dreams.* — Pedro Calderon de la Barca

BEYOND GRAMMAR
a few small thoughts

Most written clauses express statements, for example when making a legal point, presenting an argument, or leading a philosophical discussion. However, in everday language the situation is rather different. If you were to record everything you said during a day, how many whole sentences would there be? Most utterances consist merely of short phrases, questions and answers, idioms, slang, imperatives, or even single words: *you coming? not yet, what a huge car, could be worse, get in, oh wow, yeah right let's go, hmm.* In slang, dialect, and common communication, long grammatically correct sentences are the exception rather than the rule, and grammarians have only relatively recently started looking more carefully into everyday language. Only recently too has the science of grammar finally broken free from natural tongues through the study of artificial languages such as Esperanto, computer languages (pioneered by Alan Turing), and the linguistic interpretation of other information such as DNA.

Modern grammar has two branches. The first uses mathematical and computational techniques to delve into how information is coded and codes interpreted. How can information be translated from one medium

01001101011011110111001101110100000100000011011101110010011010010111010001100100110010
10110111000100000011000110110110001000000101101010110011011001010111001100100000001110
01010101110000011100000111001001100101011100110110110011001000000111001101101110100001100010
11101000110010101101010110010101101101100111011010001100110010011000010000001100110011011111
011100100010000000110010010111100001100000101101101011100000110110001001010001000000111
01110110100001100101011011100010000001101101010110000101101010110110010111011100110011100
10000001100001001000000110110001100101011001101100001011010110110000010000001100001101
11011101001011011001110100000101100001000000111000001100100110010101110011011011001010101011

to another? Is there an ideal language? Can we reduce the content of a spoken sentence to a code to translate it into any other language (a subject pioneered by Noam Chomsky). It appears that the human brain is primed at birth to learn language and grammar quickly, so a child who has not been exposed to language by the age of four will never learn to speak properly. There seems to be something common to all human minds in structuring thoughts, something categoric, involving elemental differentiations between substance, action, space, and time.

The second modern approach to grammar is more humanistic and interaction-based, focusing on the speaker and listener. Known as Speech Act Theory, it asks *what is somebody actually doing when they say something?* Here is a minimum list of speech acts:

REPRESENTATIVES: speech acts that commit a speaker to the truth of the expressed proposition, e.g. statements in court or in a paper;

DIRECTIVES: speech acts that are to cause the hearer to take a particular action, e.g. requests, commands and advice;

COMMISSIVES: speech acts that commit a speaker to some future action, e.g. promises and oaths;

EXPRESSIVES: speech acts that express the speaker's attitudes and emotions towards the proposition, e.g. congratulations, excuses and thanks;

DECLARATIONS: speech acts that change the reality in accord with the proposition of the declaration, e.g. baptisms, pronouncing someone guilty or pronouncing off-side in football.

The science of grammar can be viewed as loose, so descriptive, or tight, so normative and prescriptive, or it may be enlarged to the rules and devices governing communication and persuasion on a larger scale, in which case we enter the realms of logic and rhetoric, the subjects of two further books in this series.

APPENDIX - VERB ASPECTS

Each of these verb aspects may be associated with specific verb endings in one or more world langauges.

ACCIDENTAL: 'I happened to knock over the chair'

ATTENUATIVE: A low-intensity action. 'It glimmered'.

COMPLETIVE: An action which takes place. 'He spoke'.

CONATIVE: Attempting. 'I was trying to get to work'.

CONCLUSIVE: Like the durative (below), but terminates with a static sequel in the perfective. 'I had slept for a while'.

CONTINUATIVE: Indicates an indefinite span of time or movement with a specified direction. 'I am still eating'.

CONTINUOUS: Ongoing. 'I am eating' or 'I know'.

CURSIVE: Describes progression in a line through time / space. 'He ran across the field'.

DEFECTIVE: An action short of completion. 'I almost fell'.

DELIMITATIVE: Temporal boundaries. 'I slept for an hour'.

DISTRIBUTIVE: Expresses a distributed manipulation of objects or performance of actions. 'He chopped off their heads one after another'.

DURATIVE: Expresses an indefinite span of time, a non-locomotive uninterrupted continuum. 'I slept for while'.

EPISODIC: Something happened regularly, but not gnomically. 'John rode his bike to work in the morning'.

EXPERIENTIAL: Indicates a previous experience of performing the action. 'I have gone to school many times'.

FREQUENTATIVE: Implies repeated action. 'It sparkled', rather than 'It sparked'. Or, 'I run around', vs. 'I run'.

GNOMIC/GENERIC: Expresses a general truth. 'Fish swim and birds fly'.

HABITUAL: A subtype of imperfective, expressing a habitual tendency. 'I used to walk home from work', 'I walk home from work every day'.

IMPERFECTIVE 'I am walking to work' (progressive) or 'I walk to work every day' (habitual). An ongoing action: combining progressive and habitual aspects.

INCEPTIVE or INGRESSIVE: The beginning of a new action (as opposed to the Inchoative). 'I started to run'.

INCHOATIVE: Focuses on the beginning of a new state (as opposed to the Inceptive). 'She began to turn green'.

INTENSIVE: Indicates a high-intensity action. 'He glared'.

INTENTIONAL: Tells us something about the reasons for the action. 'I listened carefully'.

ITERATIVE: Expresses the same action repeated several times. 'I read the same books again and again'.

MODERATIVE: Indicates a medium-intensity action. 'It flowed', rather than 'It trickled' (Attenuative) or 'It gushed' (Intensive).

MOMENTANE: Describes a short-lived or sudden action. 'The mouse squeaked once' (contrasted to 'The mouse squeaked / was squeaking').

PAUSATIVE: Indicates a break in an ongoing action which frames the verb. 'I stopped working for a while'.

PERDURATIVE: An action extended beyond its wonted (or desired) length of time. 'He talked & talked & talked…'.

PERFECT (a common conflation of aspect and tense): Brings attention to the consequences of a situation in the past. 'I have arrived'.

PERFECTIVE: 'I arrived at work'. An event viewed in its entirety, without reference to internal temporal structure.

PROGRESSIVE: Describes an ongoing and evolving action. 'I am eating'.

PROSPECTIVE (a conflation of aspect and tense): Brings attention to the anticipation of a future situation. 'I am about to eat', 'I am going to eat'.

PROTRACTIVE: Indicates an action which takes a very long time, perhaps much longer than normal. 'The argument went on and on'.

PUNCTUAL: An action which happened once. 'I died'.

RECENT PERFECT, or 'after perfect'. A recently completed action. 'I just ate' or 'I am after eating' (Hiberno-English).

REPETITIVE: Indicates a continuum of repeated acts or a connected series of acts. 'We were constantly shaking hands at the wedding'.

RESUMPTIVE: 'I went back to sleep'.

REVERSATIVE: Directional change. 'He turned them back'.

REVERSIONARY: Indicates a return to a previous state or location. 'They went back to the way they were'.

SEMELFACTIVE: like Punctual, 'I sneeze'.

SERIATIVE: Indicates an interconnected series of successive separate and distinct acts. No real English equivalent.

STATIVE: Establishes an ongoing, but not evolving, state of affairs (a subtype of Continuous). 'I know French'.

TERMINAL: An inherently terminal action. 'He stopped it'.

TERMINATIVE, or cessative: 'I finished eating'.

TRANSITIONAL: Indicates a shift from one state to another. 'He was becoming angry'.